The stories about Benjamin Franklin in this book are true.  Franklin's words are not always the exact same words he used when he was alive.

Benjamin Franklin.
Born January 17, 1706 ★ Died April 17, 1790

A Book About
Benjamin Franklin

by Ruth Belov Gross
Illustrated by Anna DiVito

Scholastic Inc.
New York Toronto London Auckland Sydney

My thanks to Dr. David Hawke, Professor of History,
Herbert H. Lehman College of The City University of New York,
for the advice and help he gave me; and to
The New York Public Library for making available the
facilities of the Frederick Lewis Allen Memorial Room.

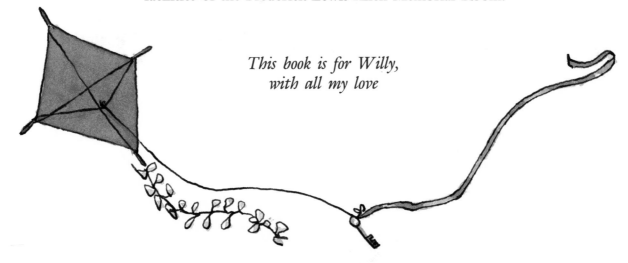

*This book is for Willy,
with all my love*

ISBN 0-590-33739-4

Text copyright © 1975 by Ruth Belov Gross.
Illustrations copyright © 1994 by Scholastic Inc.
All rights reserved. Published by Scholastic Inc.

12 11 10 9 8 7 6 5 4 3 2 1   3 4 5 6 7 8/9

Printed in the U.S.A.   08

First Scholastic printing, April 1994

Many years ago, there was a family named Franklin. They lived in Boston, in the American colony of Massachusetts.

There were eleven children in the family — five girls and six boys. Then, on a snowy January day, another baby boy was born.

Abiah Franklin looked at her new baby and smiled. She thought of a little poem she knew —

A child that's born on the Sabbath day
Is fair and wise and good and gay.

The Sabbath day — that meant Sunday, didn't it? Well, today was Sunday! Abiah hoped her new little baby would be happy and good all his life.

Together, Abiah and her husband Josiah gave their baby a name. They called him Benjamin.

From the very beginning, Benjamin was the smartest of all the Franklin children. He could read when he was five, and he could write by the time he was seven. When he was eight years old, his parents sent him to school.

In those days, many children never went to school at all. Some went for a year or two, and then they started working. Only a very few children ever went to college.

The Franklins wanted Ben to go to college. But they knew they would never be able to afford it. So when Ben was ten years old, his father took him out of school.

Ben went to work in his father's shop, making soap and candles. He never went to school again.

Ben's father would often ask friends to come over and eat with the family.

He invited people who knew a lot and who were good talkers. Then he got them talking about interesting subjects.

Maybe Josiah Franklin couldn't send his children to college. But he made sure they got a good education while they ate.

In school, Ben had been very good at reading, very good at writing, and not at all good at arithmetic.

Reading was what he liked to do best. And he kept on reading even when he wasn't going to school.

He read all of his father's books. He borrowed books. And whenever he had a little bit of money, he spent it on a book. Mostly he liked books that told him how to do something — how to swim, for example.

Ben could do plain swimming and he could do fancy swimming.

He could swim backwards, he could swim in a circle, he could swim under water.

He could swim with his legs tied together, and he could swim with his hands tied together.

He could even swim on his back with his hands straight up in the air.

Ben taught himself to do all these tricks. He found them in a book called *The Art of Swimming*. It was one of his favorite books.

Some things Ben didn't learn from a book. He just thought them up by himself.

One day he was flying his kite near a pond. Then he felt like going swimming instead. So he tied his kite to a pole and went in the water.

After a while Ben wanted to play with his kite again. He also wanted to keep on swimming. So he

got out of the water, untied his kite, and took it back to the pond with him.

Ben held the kite string in his hand and lay on his back. And almost before he knew it, he was having a new kind of fun. The kite was pulling him across the pond!

Once in a while Ben's ideas got him into trouble.
Ben and his friends used to fish for minnows at the
edge of a marsh. It was muddy there, and the boys
always got their feet covered with mud.

"Why don't we build a wharf to stand on?" Ben said one day. He pointed to a pile of stones nearby. Workmen were building a house with the stones.

The boys waited until it was dark. Then they took the stones, one by one, and built a wharf. The stones were heavy. But at last the wharf was finished.

In the morning, the workmen looked for their stones — and they found the wharf. They were angry, and they told Ben's father.

Ben tried to tell his father that the wharf was useful. Josiah Franklin punished Ben anyway. He said if something wasn't honest, it wasn't useful.

Ben went swimming and fishing whenever he could.

Most of the time, though, he had to work in his father's shop. He cut wicks for candles. He filled candle molds with wax. He helped his father boil soap in big tubs. And he hated every minute of it.

Josiah Franklin thought Ben might be happier doing some other work. So he took Ben to visit a carpenter.

Ben watched the carpenter and said he didn't want to be a carpenter. So Josiah took Ben to visit a bricklayer.

Ben watched the bricklayer and said he didn't want to be a bricklayer. So Josiah took him to see some more workers.

But Ben said he didn't want to do any of the things these men did. He wanted to be a sailor.

Josiah had to think hard now. If he didn't find something Ben liked, Ben might run away to sea. Well, Ben did like to read. Reading — that was it! If Ben liked to read, he might make a good printer.

At first Ben said he didn't want to be a printer either. But his brother James had a printing shop, and finally Ben said he would go to work for him. He was 12 years old now.

Many years later, Benjamin Franklin said he was glad his father had taken him to visit all the different workmen.

After seeing them work, he said, he always liked watching good workmen use their tools. And the things he learned from watching had come in handy whenever he had to fix something around the house or make something he needed.

Ben worked in his brother's printing shop every day except Sunday.

At lunchtime, when the other workers went out to eat, Ben would stay in the shop to study and read.

On Sunday, when the shop was quiet, Ben would go back again to study and read.

And early in the morning and late at night, Ben would study and read some more.

He taught himself how to write good sentences, and he made up poems to help himself learn new words.

He even taught himself arithmetic. In school he had been terrible at arithmetic. Now he felt ashamed that he couldn't add and subtract and multiply and divide. So he got an arithmetic book and went through the whole book by himself.

Ben soon learned to be a good printer. But he didn't like working for his brother James.

James was mean and bossy. Often he got mad at Ben and hit him. James was nine years older than Ben, and he thought Ben should do what he said.

Ben wanted to write for the newspaper James printed. He knew, though, that James wouldn't print anything of his. So he wrote some letters and signed them with a name he made up — *Silence Dogood*. And at night he slipped the letters under the door of the printing shop.

James thought the letters were interesting and funny. He printed them all. Then Ben told James who wrote the letters. James was madder at Ben than ever.

About a year later, Ben ran away from Boston. He was 17 years old.

Ben sold some of his books so he'd have a little money, and then he got on a boat for New York.

On the way, the sailors caught some fish and fried them. How good they smelled! Ben was hungry, and he wanted some.

But he didn't eat fish or meat any more. He had read a book that said it was wrong to eat animals. "They don't hurt us," Ben would say. "So why should we eat them?"

If only the fish didn't smell so good! Ben thought for a while. Then he remembered something. When the sailors were cutting the fish, he had seen small fish inside the big fish.

"Ha!" said Ben. "Fish eat fish. So why can't I?" And he had a good fish supper. Afterwards he said, "Isn't it nice to find a reason for everything you want to do?"

When Ben got to New York, he looked for a job. He could not find one, so he left for Philadelphia, in the colony of Pennsylvania.

He walked part of the way, and part of the way he went by boat. The trip took about a week. There were no trains or automobiles in those days.

Ben arrived in Philadelphia early on a Sunday morning. He was tired and dirty — and very hungry.

He walked until he found a baker's shop.

"Give me a biscuit, please," he said to the baker. He had bought biscuits many times in Boston.

"We don't make biscuits in Philadelphia," the baker said.

"Then give me a threepenny loaf of bread," Ben said.

"We don't have a threepenny loaf here," the baker said.

"Then give me three pennies' worth of ANYTHING," Ben said.

The baker gave Ben three big puffy rolls. Ben put a puffy roll under each arm and walked on, eating the third roll as he went.

By the time Ben had eaten one roll, he was full. He was glad to give the rest of his bread to a hungry woman and her child.

Soon after Ben came to Philadelphia, he found a job and a place to stay.

He was hired by a printer, and he lived next door to the printing shop in the house of Mr. and Mrs. Read. Their daughter Deborah was about Ben's age.

One day when Ben was at work, the governor of Pennsylvania came to the printing shop. He had heard about Ben, and he had come especially to see him.

The governor said a good printer like Ben should have his own printing shop. And he told Ben to go to London and pick out the things he would need to start a shop. The governor promised to write letters to people in London, to tell them that he would pay for everything Ben bought.

Ben went to London. But the governor never did write the letters!

Ben did the only thing he could do. He got a job as a printer. He stayed in London for a year and a half, and then he went back to Philadelphia.

Ben went back to Philadelphia when he was 20 years old. A year or so later he borrowed some money and opened his own printing shop.

Then he started his own newspaper. He called it *The Pennsylvania Gazette*. Now he had a newspaper and a printing shop.

Not long after that, Ben married Deborah Read. Debby teased Ben about his first day in Philadelphia, when he walked down the street eating his puffy roll. "I saw you then," she said, "but you didn't see me."

Debby helped Ben run a little store in the printing shop. They sold all sorts of things there. They sold slates and writing paper, pens and pencils, tea and coffee, mustard and cheese — and soap that Ben's family made.

By the time Benjamin Franklin was 25 years old, he had a printing shop, a newspaper, and a store. He was married, and he had a baby son, William.

Ben Franklin worked hard, and he wanted everybody to know it.

When he had a load of paper to take to his shop, he put it in a wheelbarrow. Then he pushed the wheelbarrow through the streets so everybody could see him.

"There goes Ben Franklin," people would say. "How hard he works!"

That was just what Ben wanted them to say.

One day a group of Ben's friends came to see him. "Some rich men don't like what you say in your newspaper," one of them said.

"They are angry," said another.

Ben Franklin thanked his friends and invited them to his house for supper. "We can talk it over tonight," he said.

That night, Franklin's friends came for supper. What a supper! There was nothing on the table but water and some strange-looking pudding.

Franklin took a big helping of pudding and ate it. But none of his friends could swallow a single bite. The pudding looked like sawdust — and it tasted even worse.

At last Franklin finished his pudding and stood up. He was smiling.

"You can see that I am happy with very plain food," he said. "Now go and tell those rich men I don't need their money. Tell them I will go on saying what I think is right."

When Ben Franklin first came to Philadelphia, there were no good bookstores in town. People who wanted books had to write to England to get them.

So Franklin ordered books from England and sold them in his store. That way, he made it easy for people to buy books. He also made more money for himself.

Most people in the colonies couldn't buy books. Books were too expensive. But everybody — rich or poor — bought an almanac once a year.

An almanac was a special kind of calendar. It showed the months and weeks and days of the year. It told its readers when the tide would be high and when the moon would be full and what the weather would be like.

Sometimes it had jokes and poems too.

When Benjamin Franklin was 26, he decided to print his own almanac. He was sure his almanac would be better than anybody else's — and it was.

Franklin's almanac had wise and funny sayings on almost every page. Franklin wrote the sayings himself, but he pretended that they were written by a poor man named Richard Saunders — and soon his almanac was known as *Poor Richard's Almanack*.

Ben Franklin published *Poor Richard's Almanack* every year for many years. It helped make him rich and famous.

Some sayings from *Poor Richard's Almanack*

March windy, and April rainy,
Makes May the pleasantest month of any.

Three may keep a Secret,
if two of them are dead.

Nothing but Money
Is sweeter than Honey.

The sleeping Fox
catches no Poultry.

A true Friend is
the best Possession.

Speak little,
do much.

The worst wheel of the cart
makes the most noise.

An Egg today is better
than a Hen to-morrow.

Fish and Visitors stink in 3 days.

When he was 42 years old, Benjamin Franklin decided he was rich enough. He told his friends he was going to stop working.

From now on, he said, he would let his partner run the printing shop, the newspaper, and the almanac. He would still get some money from them, but only enough to live on.

Franklin's friends were puzzled. "Don't you want more money?" they would ask.

"I have enough for my family," Franklin would say. "Why do I need more?" And then he would tell his friends this story.

One day, he said, he visited a man who lived by himself in a big house. The man's living room was big enough for five families. The table in the dining room was big enough for 25 people.

"Why do you have such a big living room?" Franklin asked.

"Because I can afford it," the man said.

"Why do you have such a big dining-room table?" Franklin asked.

"Because I can afford it," the man said.

Every time Franklin asked the man why something was so big, the man said he could afford it.

Finally Franklin said, "Then why do you wear such a small hat? I am sure you can afford a hat ten times as big as your head."

Now that Ben Franklin wasn't working any more, he could do what he wanted.

Most of all, he wanted to do some scientific experiments — especially experiments with electricity.

At that time, there were no electric lights or radios or anything else that worked by electricity. Nobody knew very much about electricity then.

Franklin thought that thunderclouds might contain electricity, but he wasn't sure. He did know there were sparks whenever lightning struck a tree or a house. Was lightning the same thing as electricity?

He would try to find out.

At last Franklin thought of a way to do the experiment. He would make a kite and send it up into the clouds.

So he made the kite. And one day when a thunderstorm was coming, he took his kite out to a cow pasture. His son, who was 21 years old now, went with him.

Franklin sent his kite up into the stormy sky and waited. For a long time, nothing happened.

Suddenly some loose threads on the kite string stood straight up. Electricity was passing through the wet string!

Now Franklin touched the metal key that was tied to the string. Sparks flew from the key — electric sparks! The experiment was a success! It proved there was electricity in the storm clouds.

Franklin didn't know how dangerous his experiment really was. If a bolt of lightning had struck the kite, he and his son would have been killed. But they were lucky.

Ben Franklin was sure now that another idea of his would work — an idea for something that would protect houses from lightning. He called it a lightning rod.

Franklin was happy to tell everybody about the lightning rod. That was just like him. He didn't want any money for his ideas. If his ideas helped others, that was all he wanted.

About ten years before this, Franklin had invented a special kind of stove for heating a room.

Everyone had fireplaces then, but people had to stand close to the fire to get warm. Even so, they would be warm in front and cold in back — "scorched before and froze behind," Franklin said.

Franklin's stove was something like a metal box that fit inside the fireplace. It made the whole room warm. And it used less wood than a regular fireplace did.

Benjamin Franklin could have sold the idea for his stove if he had wanted to. Instead, he gave the idea away free.

The inventions of many people had helped him, he said — and now he was glad to help others with the things he invented.

Benjamin Franklin was 46 years old now, and he was happy.

He had made the experiment with his kite that year, and it had been a success.

He had as much money as he needed. He had many friends, a loving wife, a big son of 21, and a very dear daughter of nine. Her name was Sarah, but everyone called her Sally.

The only thing that made Franklin sad was the memory of his little son Francis. Francis was only four when he died.

Franklin laughed a lot, and he made his friends laugh too.

Once a neighbor asked him for some advice. "I have a barrel of beer behind my house," the neighbor said. "But people keep helping themselves. How can I stop the thieves from drinking my beer?"

"That's easy," said Franklin. "Put a barrel of good wine next to the beer. The thieves will like the wine so much they'll leave your beer alone."

Ben Franklin might have been happy to read books, do his experiments, and live quietly with his family.

But the people of Philadelphia thought he would be a good person to help run the colony of Pennsylvania. They chose him to be a member of the Pennsylvania Assembly.

Then in 1753, when he was 47 years old, he became postmaster general for the 13 colonies. He shared the job with a man from Virginia. The other man was not well, though, and Ben Franklin did most of the work.

Franklin wanted to visit all the post offices in the colonies. So he got on his horse and set out.

One cold, rainy day, after hours of riding over terrible roads, Franklin came to an inn. "At last!" he thought. "I'll stop and rest by the fire for a while."

But there wasn't a seat to be had by the fireplace.

In his loudest voice, Franklin called to the inn-keeper's son. "Boy," he said, "give my horse a bucket of oysters."

The boy could not believe his ears. Horses ate oats, not oysters!

"You heard me," Franklin roared. "Get my horse a bucket of oysters!"

All the people in the room turned to look at Franklin. What kind of crazy horse did he have?

The boy ran for the oysters and took them outside to the horse. Everybody in the room ran outside too — everybody but Ben Franklin.

When the people came back, they found him sitting happily in the best chair by the fire. His horse didn't eat oysters, of course, and he knew it. But he had thought of a good way to get everybody out of the room.

Ben Franklin did a good job of running the post office.

He did a good job as a member of the Pennsylvania Assembly too.

And now the Pennsylvania Assembly decided to send him to England.

At that time, Pennsylvania and the other American colonies belonged to England. The people who lived in Pennsylvania thought they were not being treated fairly. They hoped Franklin could talk to important people in England and straighten things out.

Franklin left for England in 1757. He took his son William with him.

Franklin thought he would be in England for just one year. He stayed for five years. Then he came home to America.

Two years later, the Pennsylvania Assembly sent him to England again. This time he was away for ten years.

Ben Franklin wanted his wife to come to England. But Debby Franklin was afraid to make the boat trip across the ocean.

In London, Franklin did as much as he could to straighten things out between the Pennsylvania colony and England. He also did everything he could for the other colonies. They were having trouble with England too.

England was making the colonists pay a tax on dozens of things they used every day — things like newspapers and almanacs and school books. The tax was called the stamp tax, because people had to buy special stamps to pay it.

The colonists knew they had to pay taxes. But they wanted to decide for themselves what those taxes would be.

England would not let the colonies do that. England said it had the right to tax the colonies any way it wanted to.

Benjamin Franklin worked hard to get the stamp tax changed. He made speeches. He talked to important people. And finally it was agreed that the colonists would not have to pay the stamp tax any more.

The colonists thought Franklin was a great hero.

But many people in England, including the King of England, thought Franklin was a great trouble-maker.

Before long, England made the colonists pay some new taxes. This time the colonists had to pay a tax whenever they bought tea or paint or glass or paper.

So Benjamin Franklin stayed on in England. He wanted to stay as long as he could help the colonies.

He was homesick, though, and he missed Debby very much. Often she sent him some food from America, things she knew he liked — buckwheat flour for pancakes, and apples and dried peaches and cranberries and nuts.

Debby's packages helped Franklin feel better. "Since I cannot be in America," he wrote to her, "everything that comes from there comforts me a little, as being something like home."

Early in the year 1775, Franklin got some sad news. His Debby had died.

By then, Franklin knew that England would never give the colonies what they wanted. He had tried to make peace between the colonies and England. But he had failed. He was sure now that there would be a war, a long and terrible war.

It was time for Benjamin Franklin to go back to Philadelphia.

Franklin left England in the spring of 1775. He was 69 years old.

A year later, the colonies and England were at war. The colonies did not want to belong to England any longer. They were fighting for their freedom.

The war was called the American Revolution.

Benjamin Franklin had once hoped the war could be avoided. "There never was a good war or a bad peace," he said.

But now that the war had started, Benjamin Franklin used all the strength and all the wisdom he had to help the colonies.

Benjamin Franklin was busier now than he had ever been.

He was a member of Congress. Congress met in Philadelphia then.

He was elected postmaster general by Congress.

He was sent to Cambridge, Massachusetts, to talk to George Washington. George Washington was the commander of the army.

He went to Canada on important government business.

He was on at least ten committees of Congress. One committee had its meetings at 6 o'clock every morning!

And he was a member of the committee that was asked to write down the reasons why the colonies should no longer be ruled by England — to write the Declaration of Independence.

Thomas Jefferson was the person on the committee who did the writing. Benjamin Franklin read what Jefferson wrote and made a few changes.

"All men are created equal," the Declaration of Independence said. And it said that people have the right to start a new government when the old government takes away their safety and happiness.

On July 4, 1776, representatives of the colonies agreed to sign the Declaration of Independence.

From that time on, the colonies were not colonies any more. They were the United States of America.

The United States needed the help of other countries in the war against England. And now the Congress of the United States asked Benjamin Franklin to go to France. Franklin was supposed to make friends with the French people and the French government.

So in 1776, Benjamin Franklin went to France. He took two of his grandsons with him, six-year-old Benny and 17-year-old Temple.

Franklin was 70 years old now. He was so tired when he got to France he could hardly stand.

But soon Franklin was feeling better and working as hard as ever.

He was having as much fun as ever, too. He went to parties. He played chess with pretty women. He made up songs and sang them for his friends. He wrote funny stories and printed them on his own little printing press. He taught Benny how to swim.

Just about everybody in France loved Benjamin Franklin. They knew about his experiments with electricity, and they had read *Poor Richard's Almanack*. Almost everybody kept a picture of Franklin in the house.

Franklin said he'd better not do anything bad and have to run away. His face was so well known, he said, he'd be caught before he could go very far.

Benjamin Franklin spent nine years in France. Most of that time, the Revolutionary War was going on in America.

Franklin got France to help the United States. And with France's help, the United States won the war.

In 1785, Benjamin Franklin went home at last. He wanted to die in America. He was 79 years old now, and he was not well.

Bells were ringing and people were cheering when Benjamin Franklin stepped off the boat in Philadelphia.

He thought he could settle down now with his daughter and her husband and their children. He thought he would have time for science, and time to read, to sit in the garden, to play with his grand-children.

But he didn't have time for these things right away. Right now, in 1787, each state was sending men to Philadelphia for an important meeting. What kind of government would be best for the United States? Who would run the government? Who would make the laws? Together, the men at the meeting would decide these questions.

The state of Pennsylvania asked Benjamin Franklin to go to the meeting, and he went.

Franklin was an old man now. He had pains in his kidneys. He had to lean on a cane when he walked. But he went to the meetings every day.

The meetings went on for four months. All during the hot summer of 1787, the men talked about the kind of government they wanted.

At last they wrote down the things they had decided. And what they wrote was the Constitution of the United States.

Benjamin Franklin was the oldest man to help write the Constitution. He was 81 years old.

In 1788, eleven of the thirteen states agreed to the Constitution. In 1789, George Washington was elected the first President of the United States.

Benjamin Franklin was growing older and weaker. He spent the last year of his life in bed.

Sometimes his friends would come and read to him.

Sometimes he would write a letter. He would tell his grandson Benny what he wanted to say, and Benny would write it down.

The best part of Franklin's day was in the afternoon. Every afternoon, his nine-year-old granddaughter Deborah came to his bedside with her spelling lesson. And Franklin would listen while Deborah spelled her words.

Franklin's pains grew worse. But his mind was as good as ever. He kept on thinking about science and the experiments he could do.

Franklin made his last experiment about a year before he died. He made it one night when his family was asleep and the house was still.

He used a watch for the experiment. Could he hear it tick five feet away? Ten feet away? Twenty feet? Franklin listened carefully in the quiet house. When the watch was 20 feet away, he could barely hear it tick.

Then he put his hand behind his ear and pushed on it. He could hear much better now. He could even hear the watch ticking when he was 45 feet away!

Benjamin Franklin had a special reason for making this experiment. His friend, Mr. Small, was growing deaf. Franklin was old and weak himself, but he wanted to find a way to help his friend hear better. And he did.

Benjamin Franklin died in Philadelphia on April 17, 1790. He was 84 years old.

He had had a happy and good life. And he had lived long enough to see George Washington become President of the United States.

Thousands and thousands of people went to the funeral of Benjamin Franklin. The bells of Philadelphia were rung one last time in his honor. Then he was buried next to his beloved wife Deborah.